MONSTER

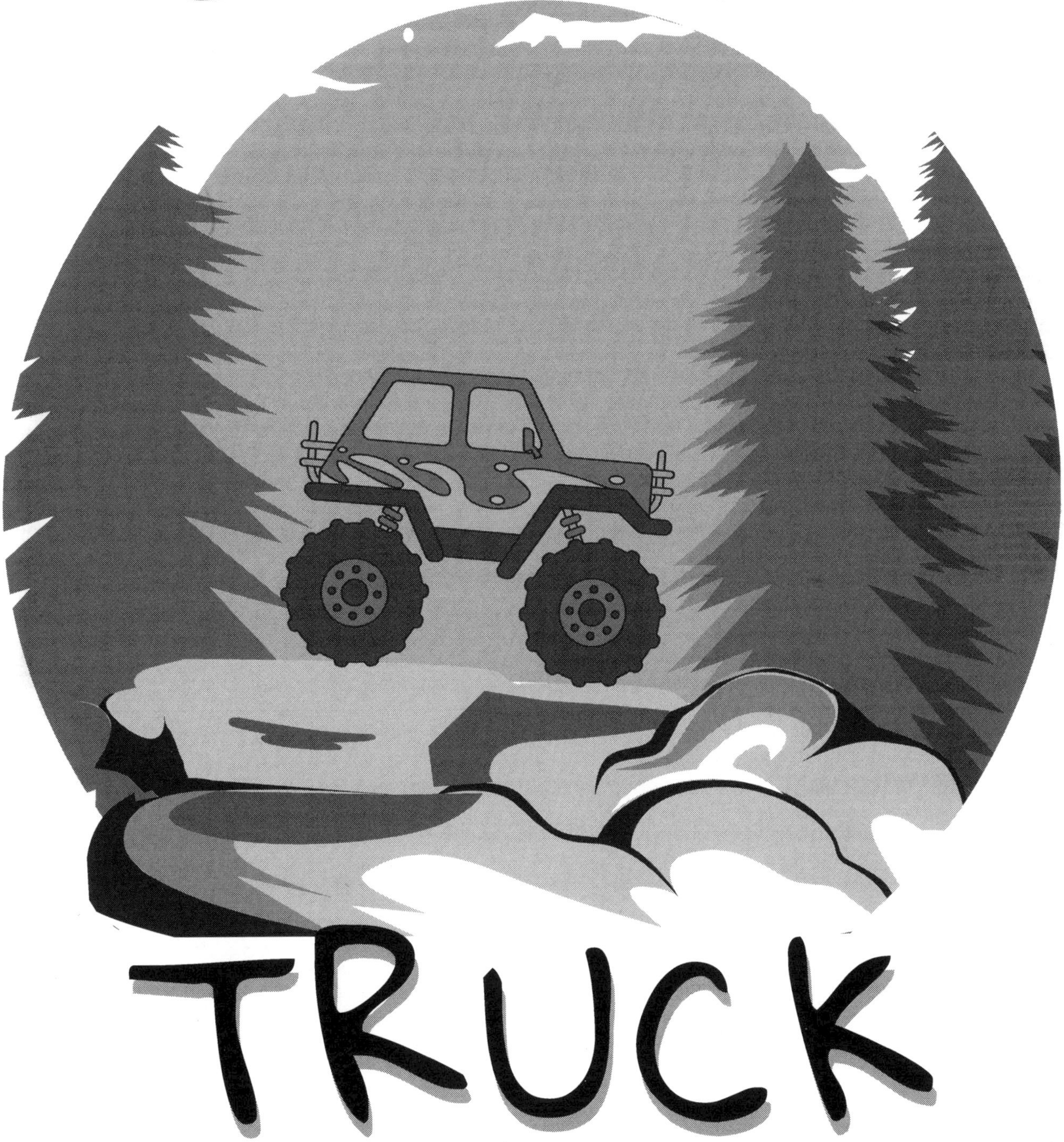

TRUCK

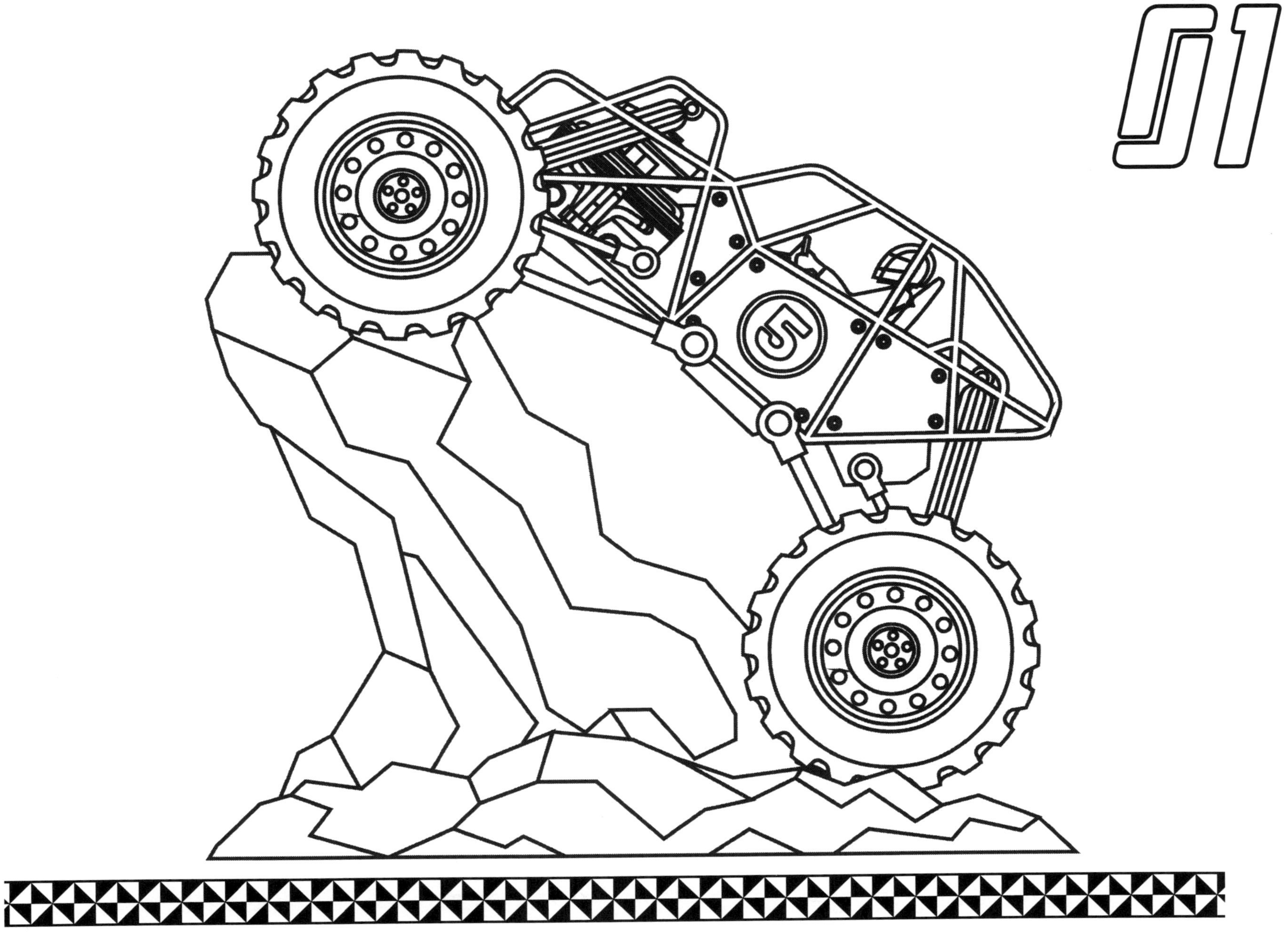

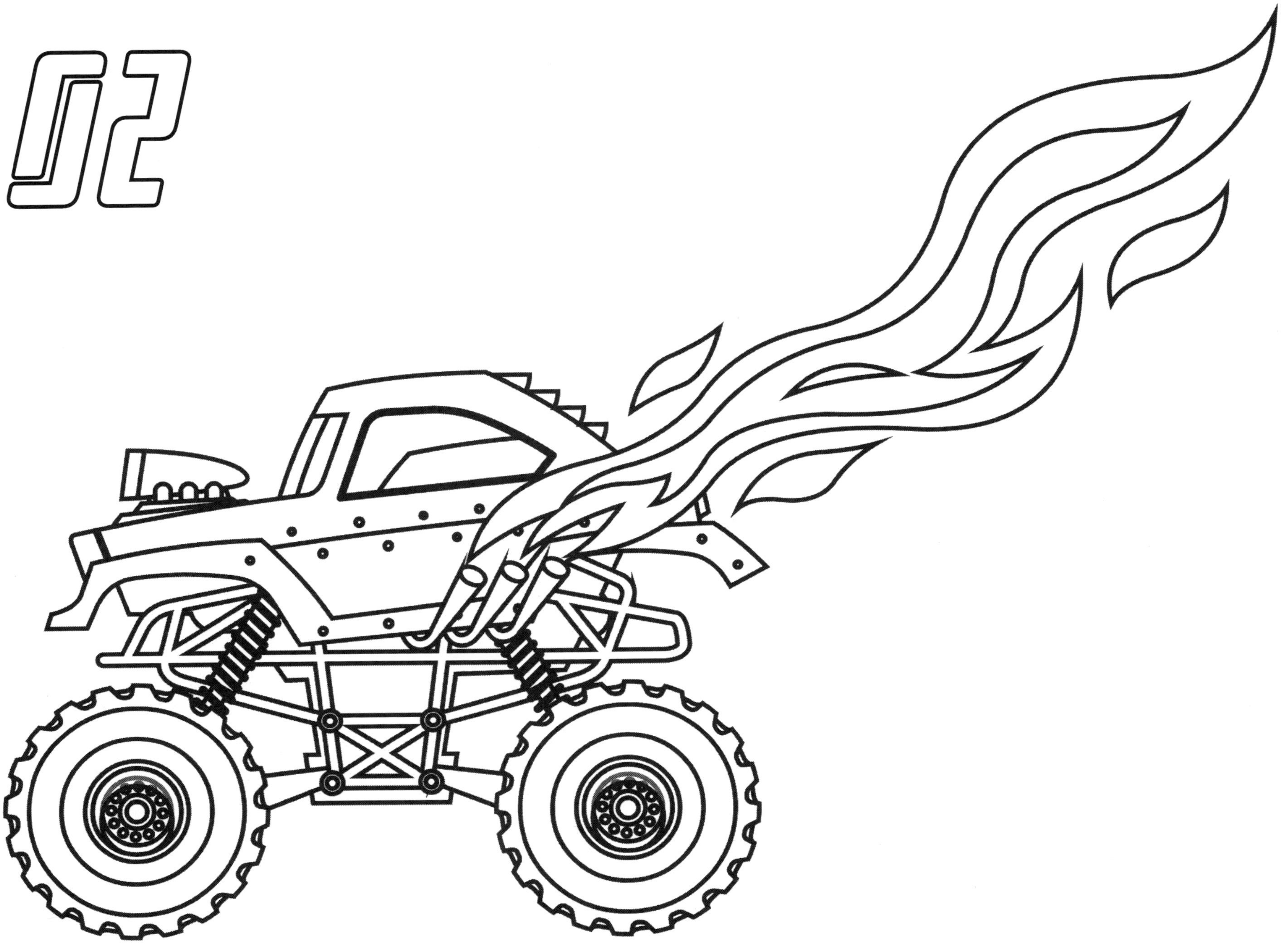

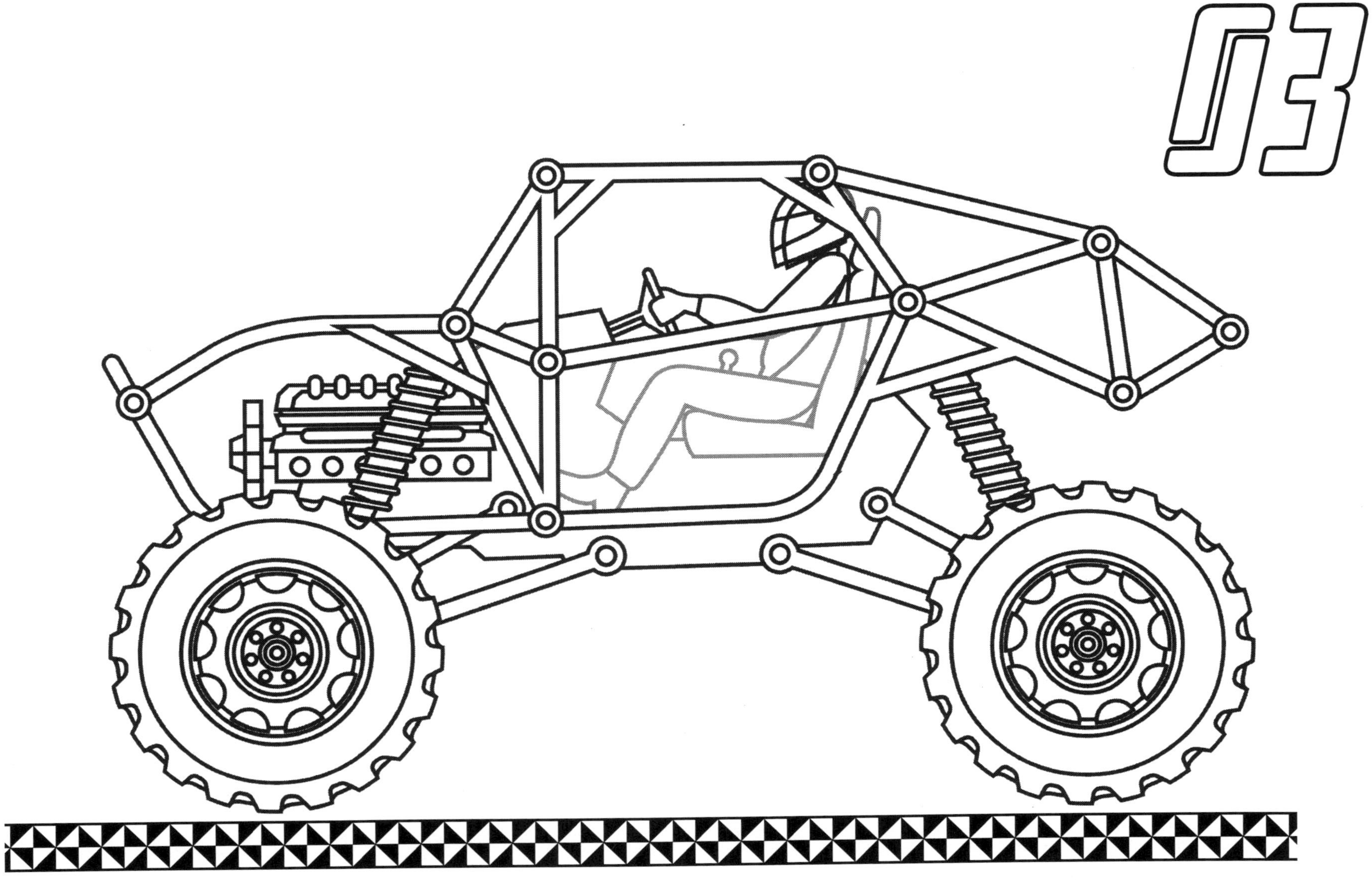
13

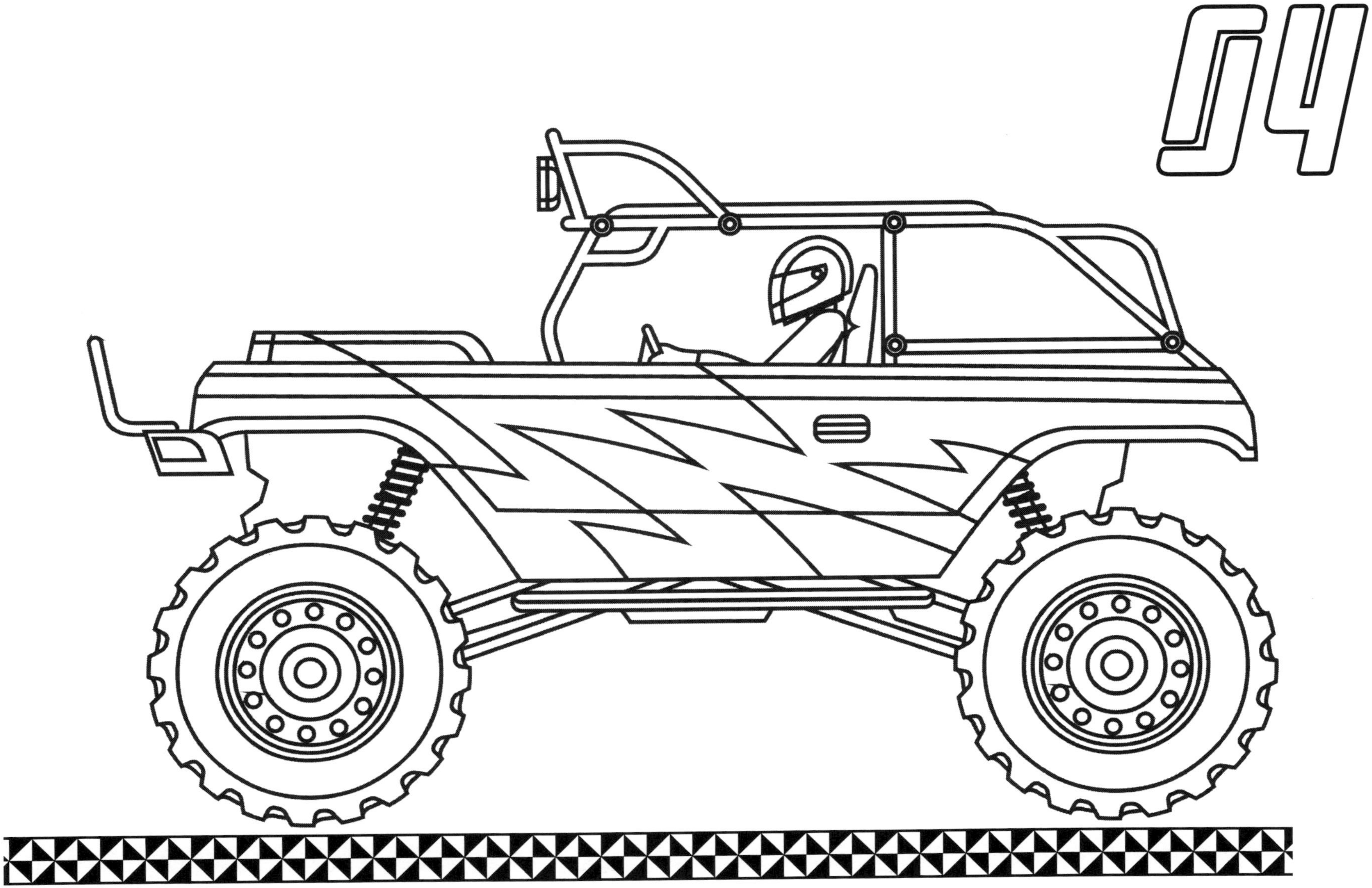
54

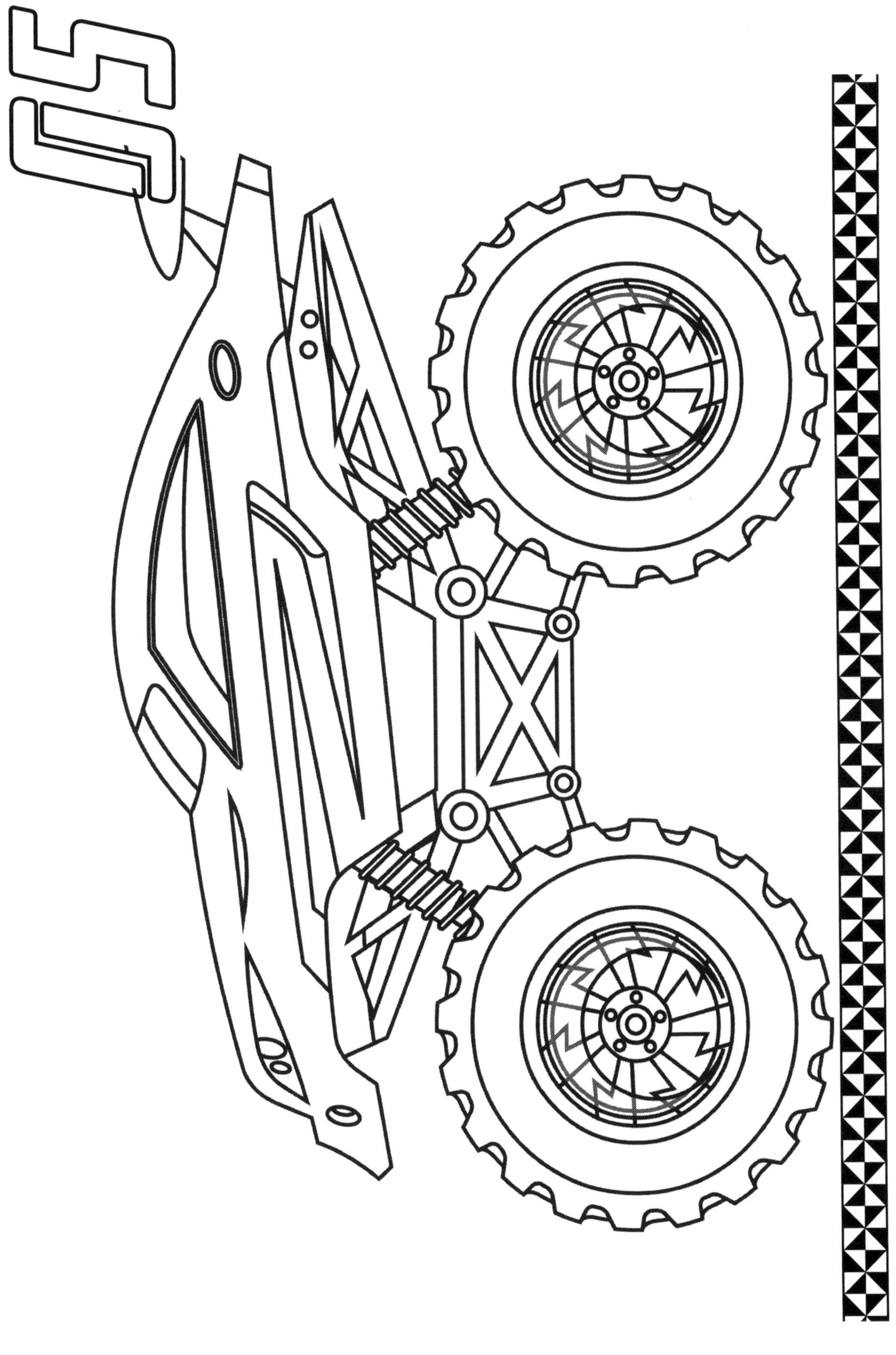

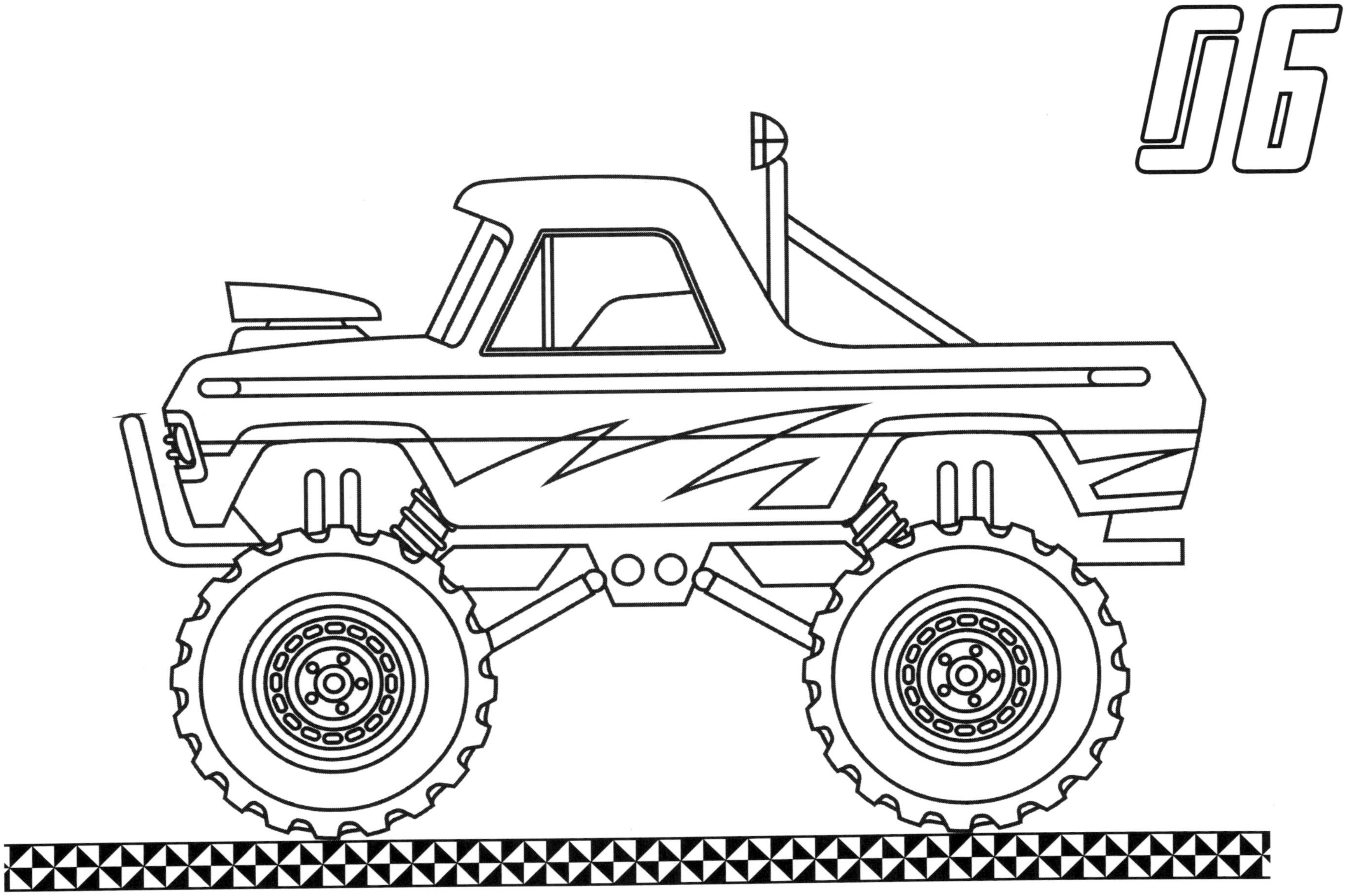

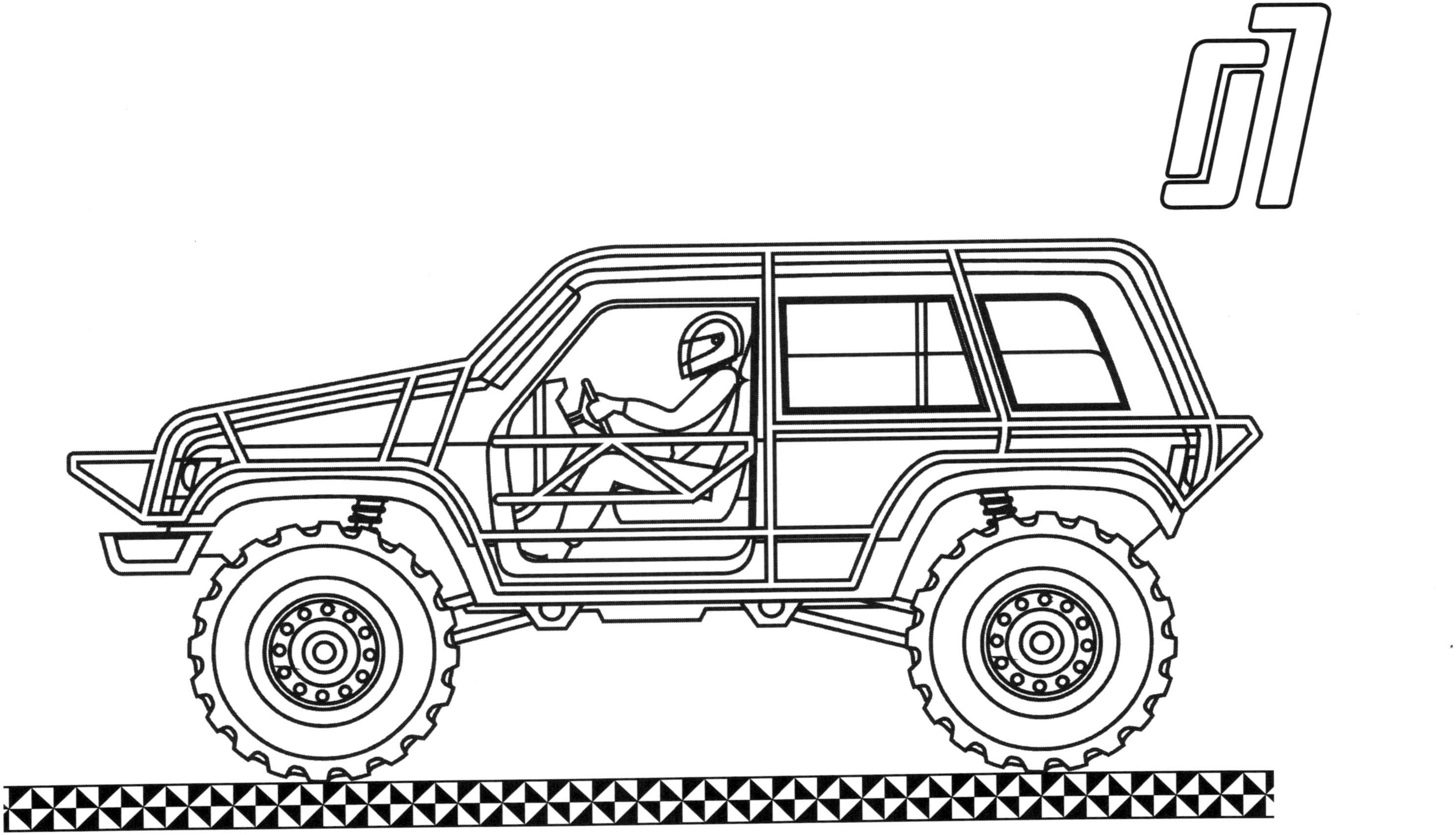

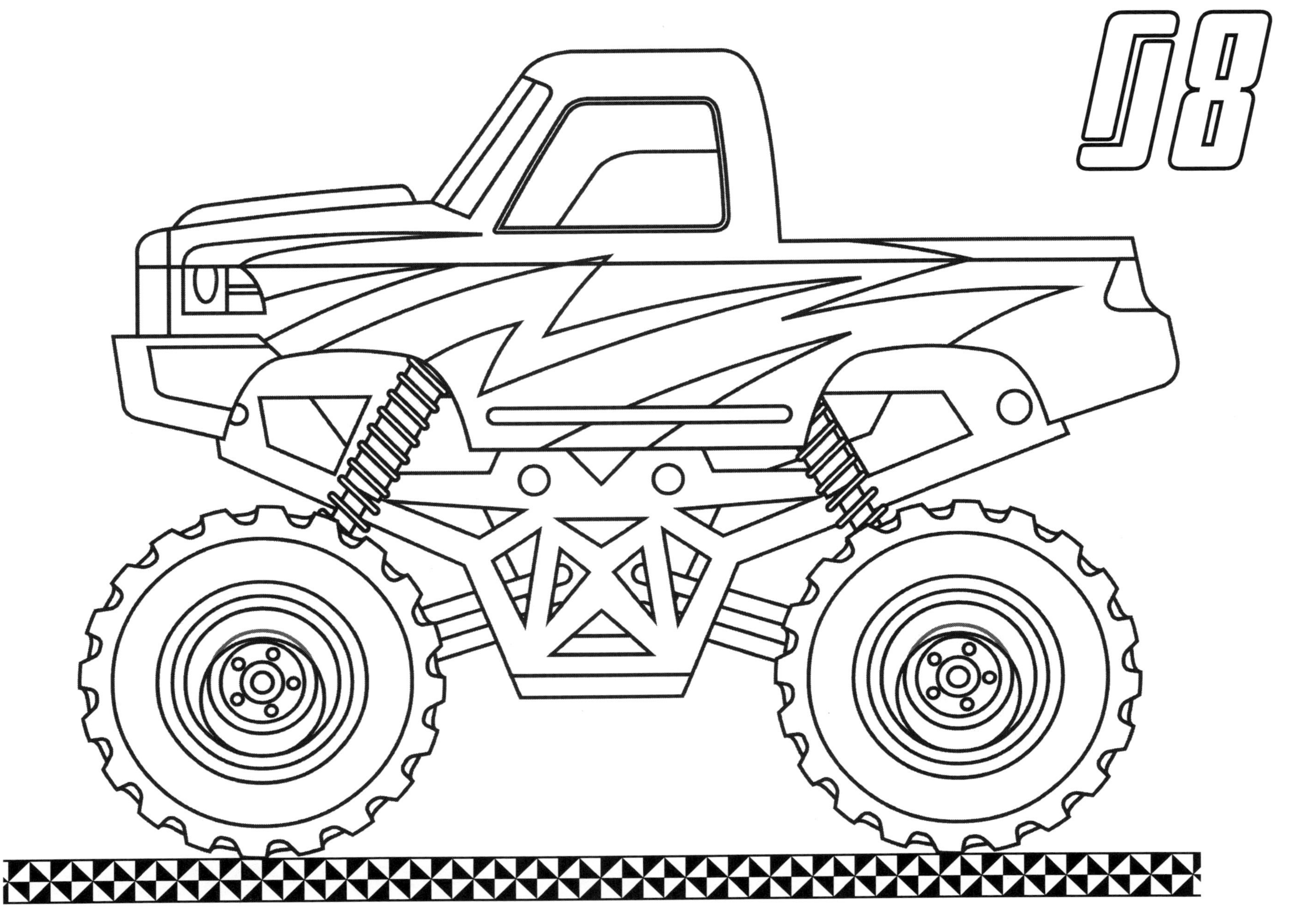

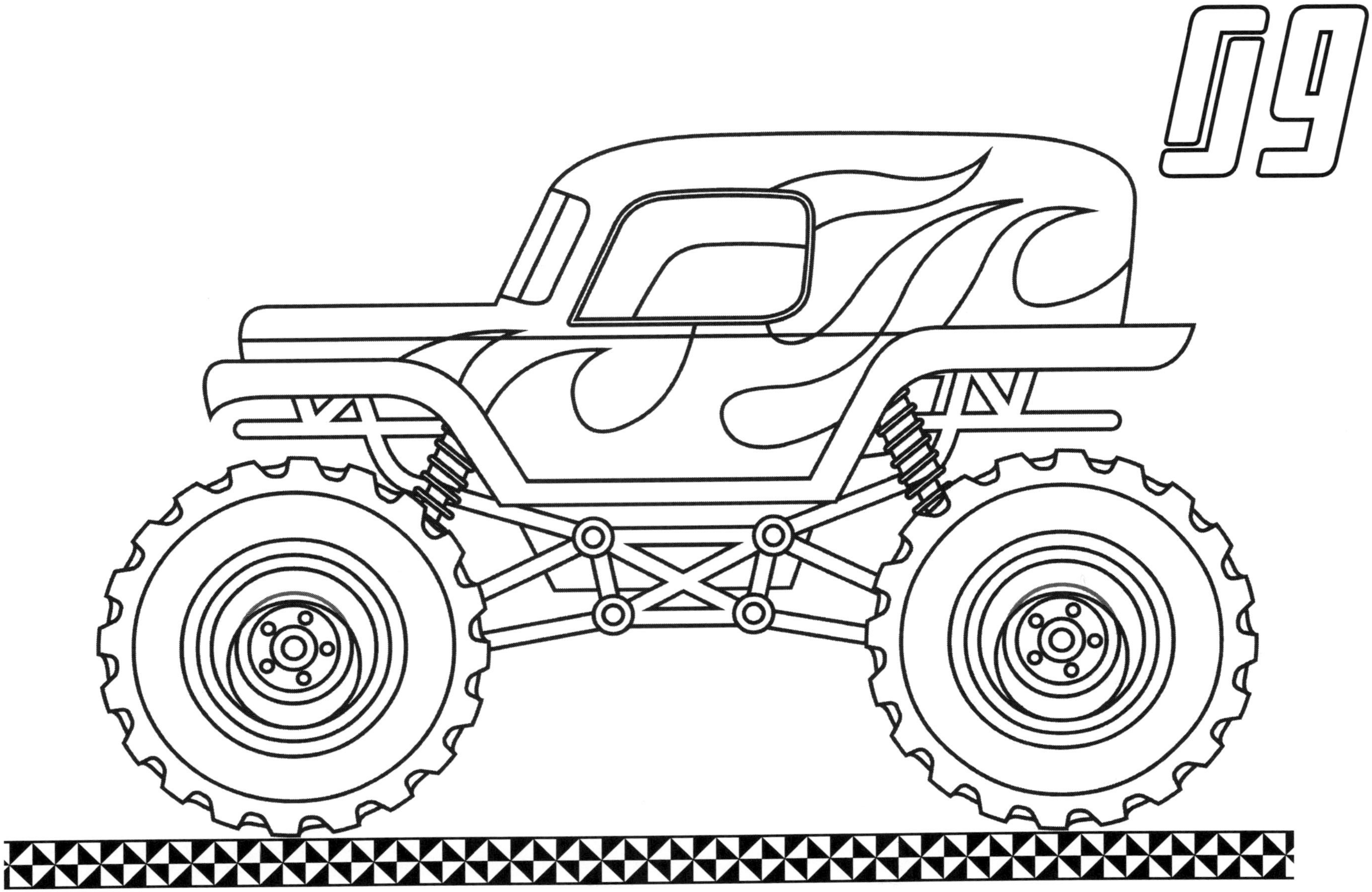
19

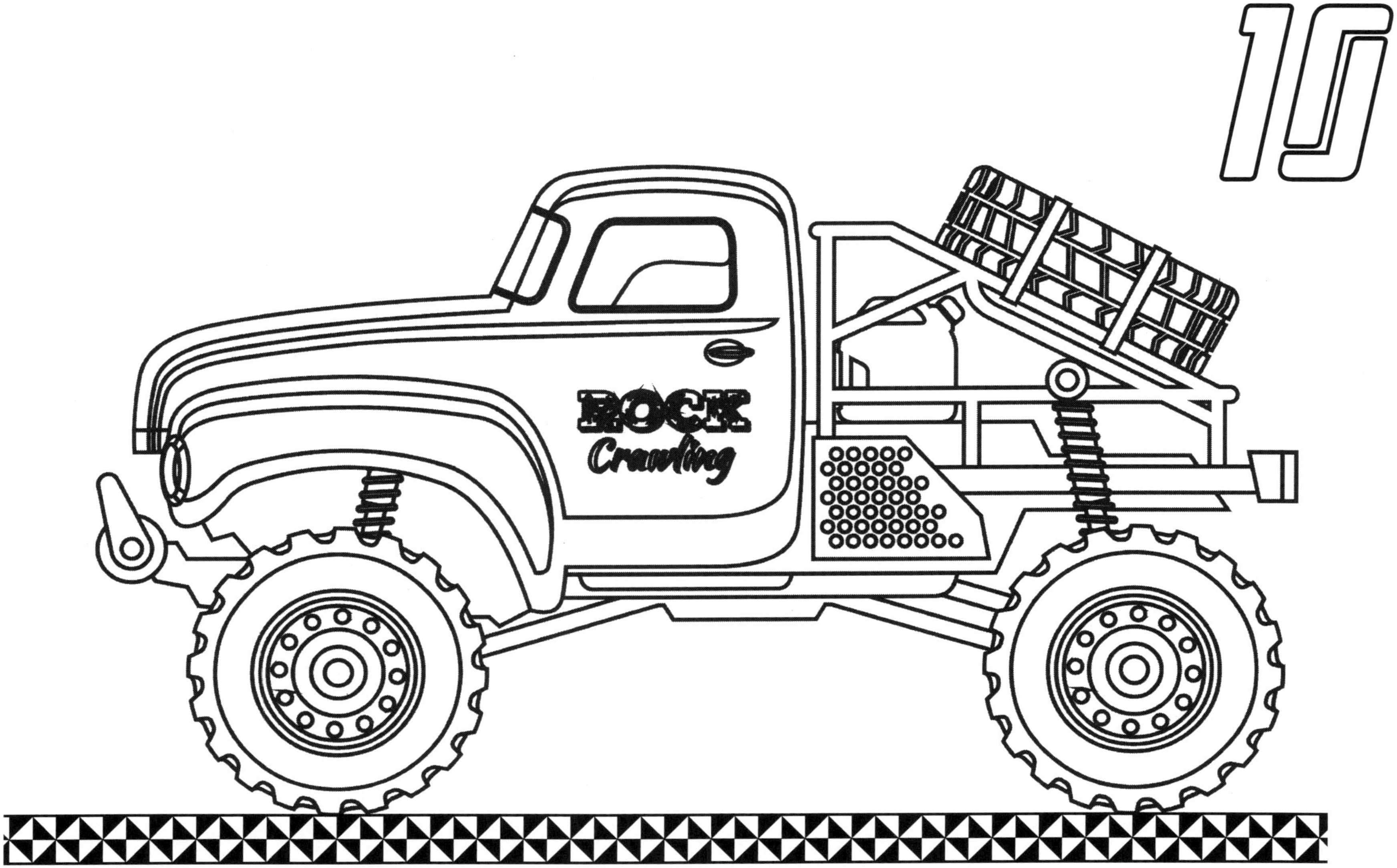
ROCK
Crawling

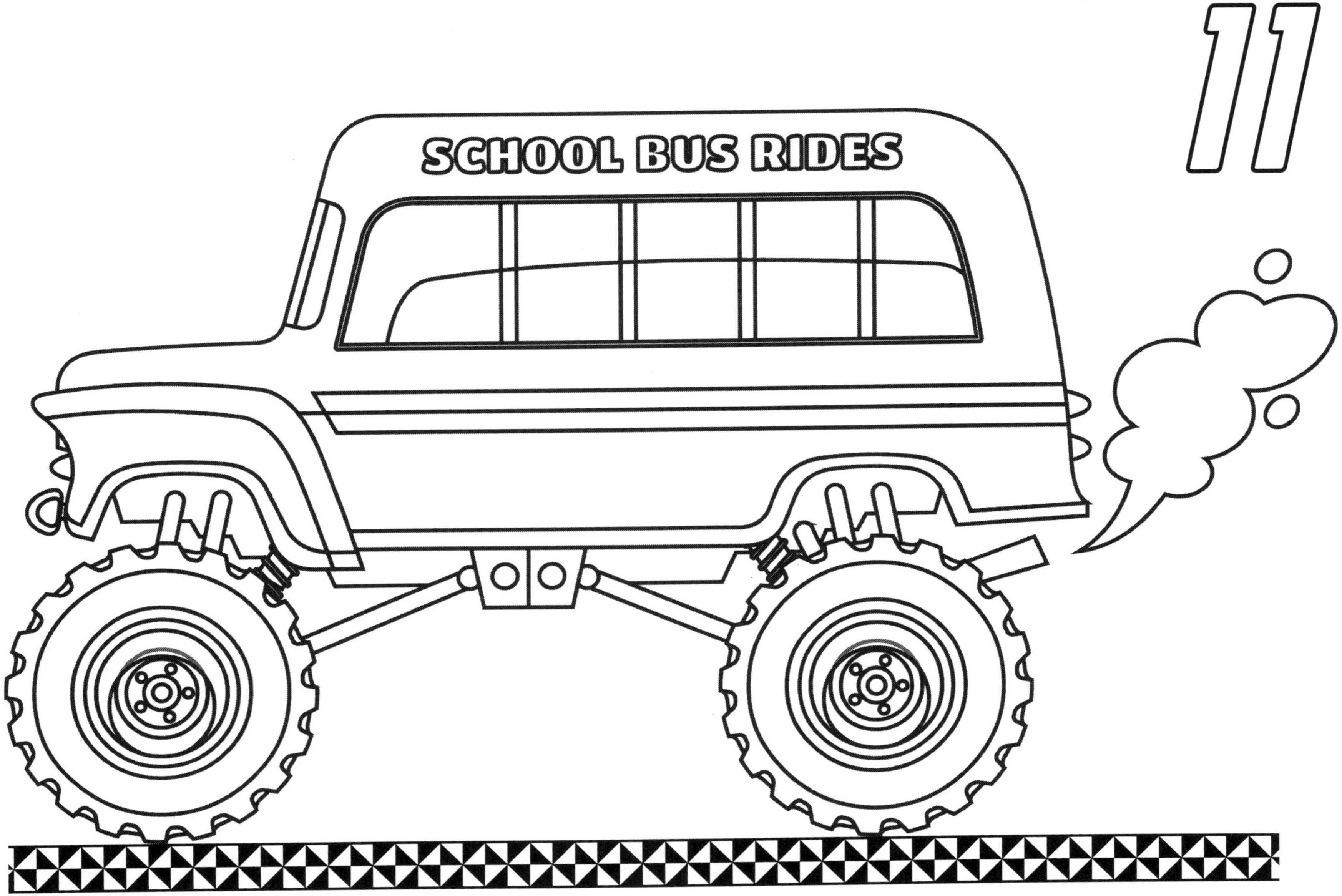
SCHOOL BUS RIDES
11

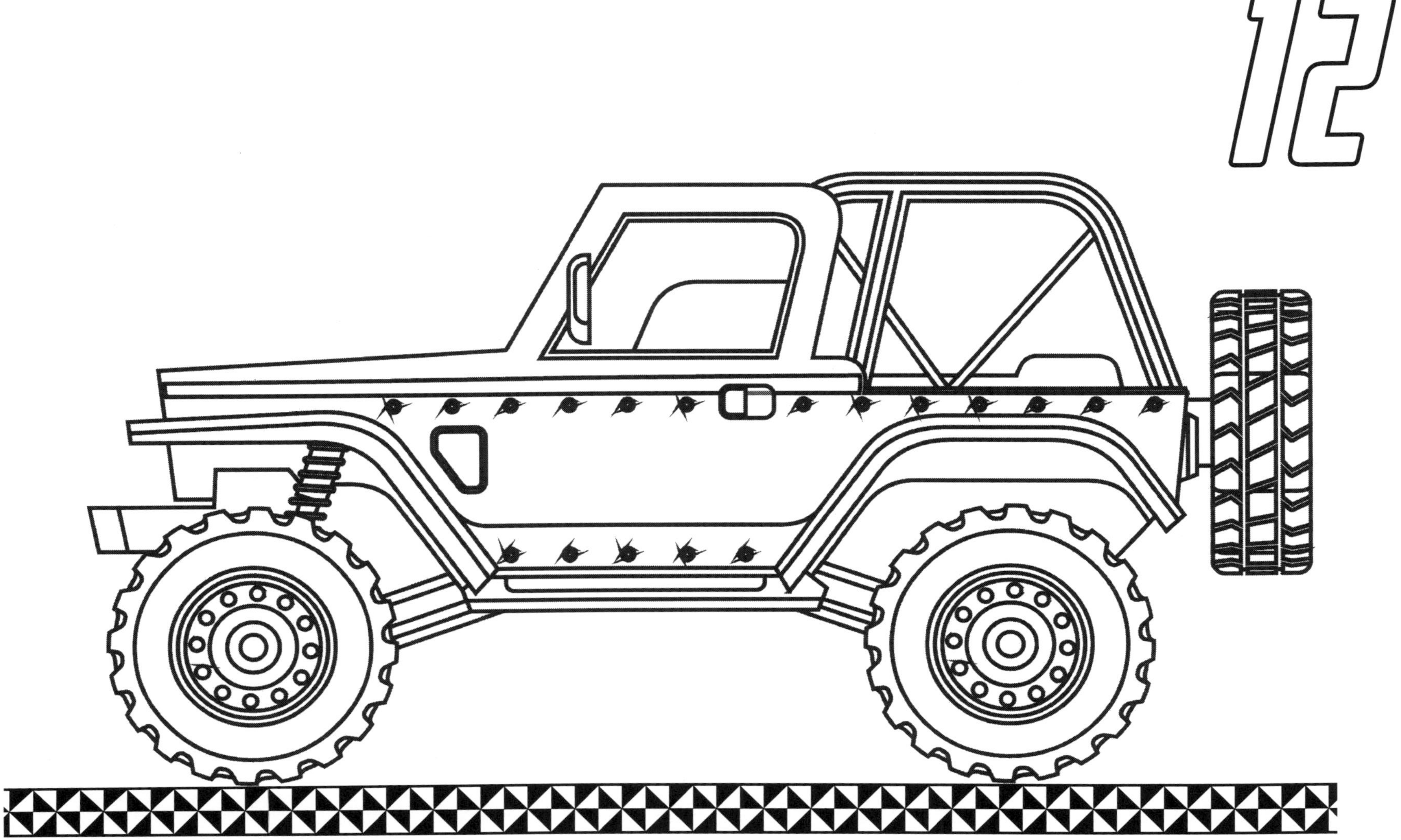
12

PART TWO

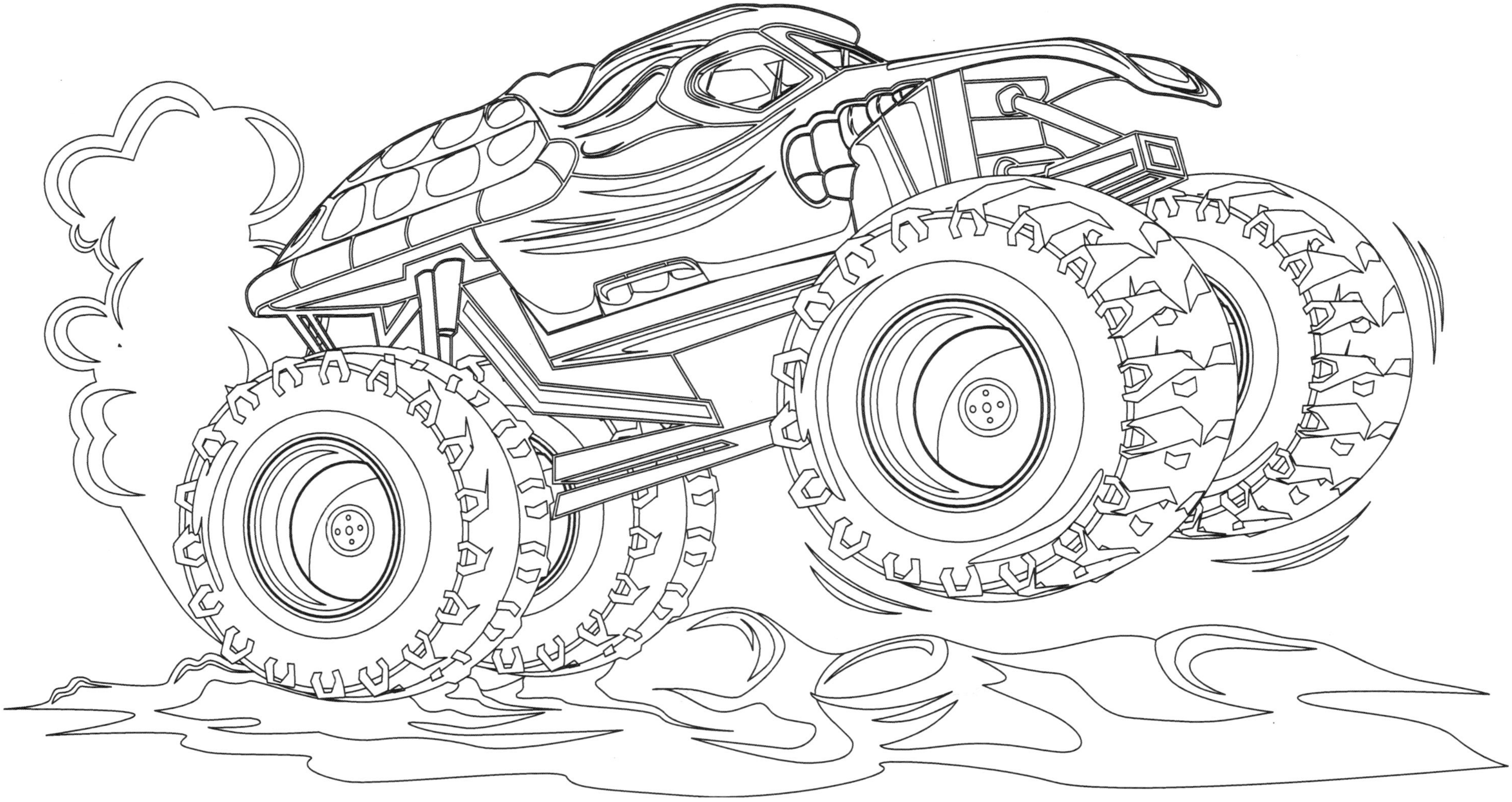

13

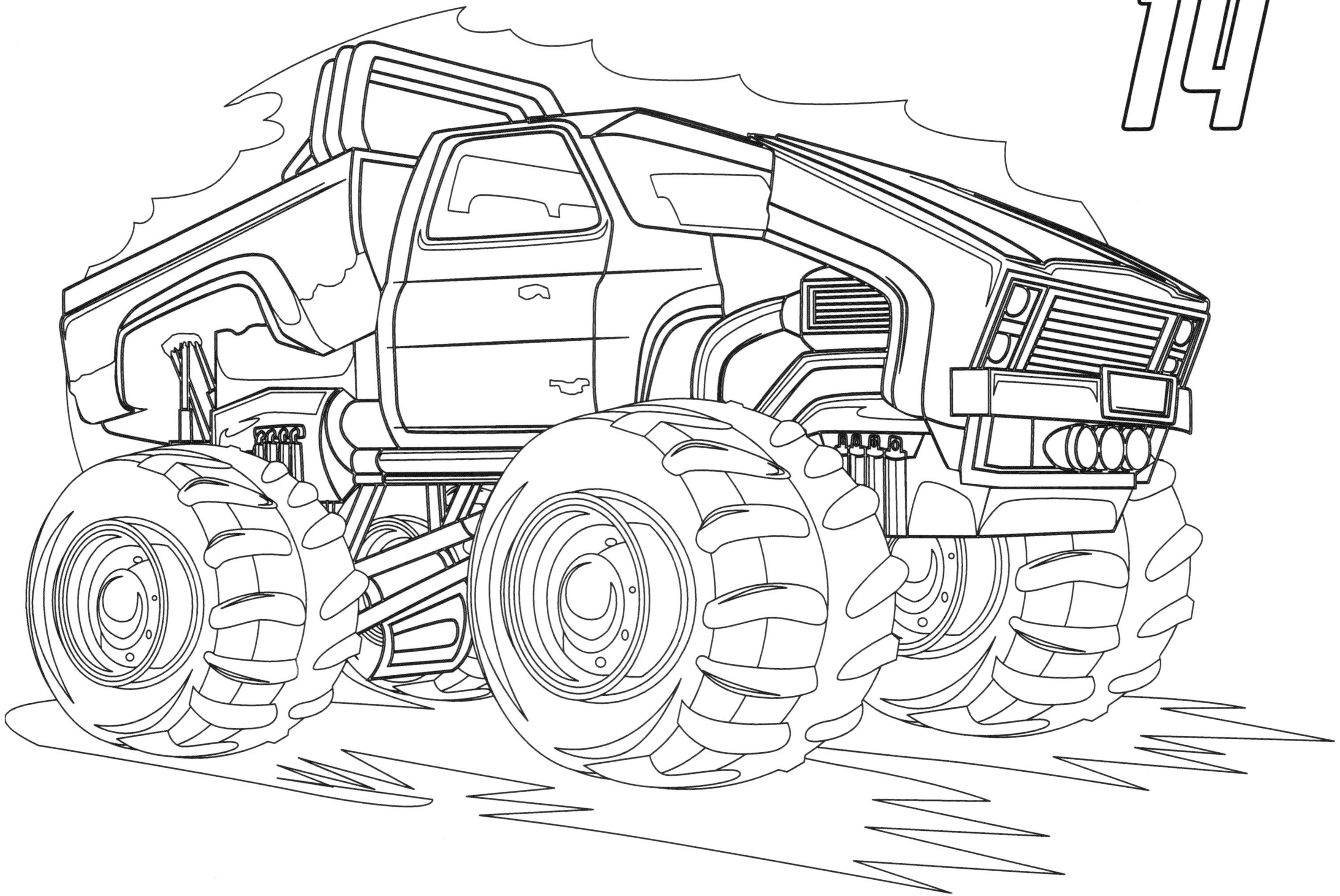

15

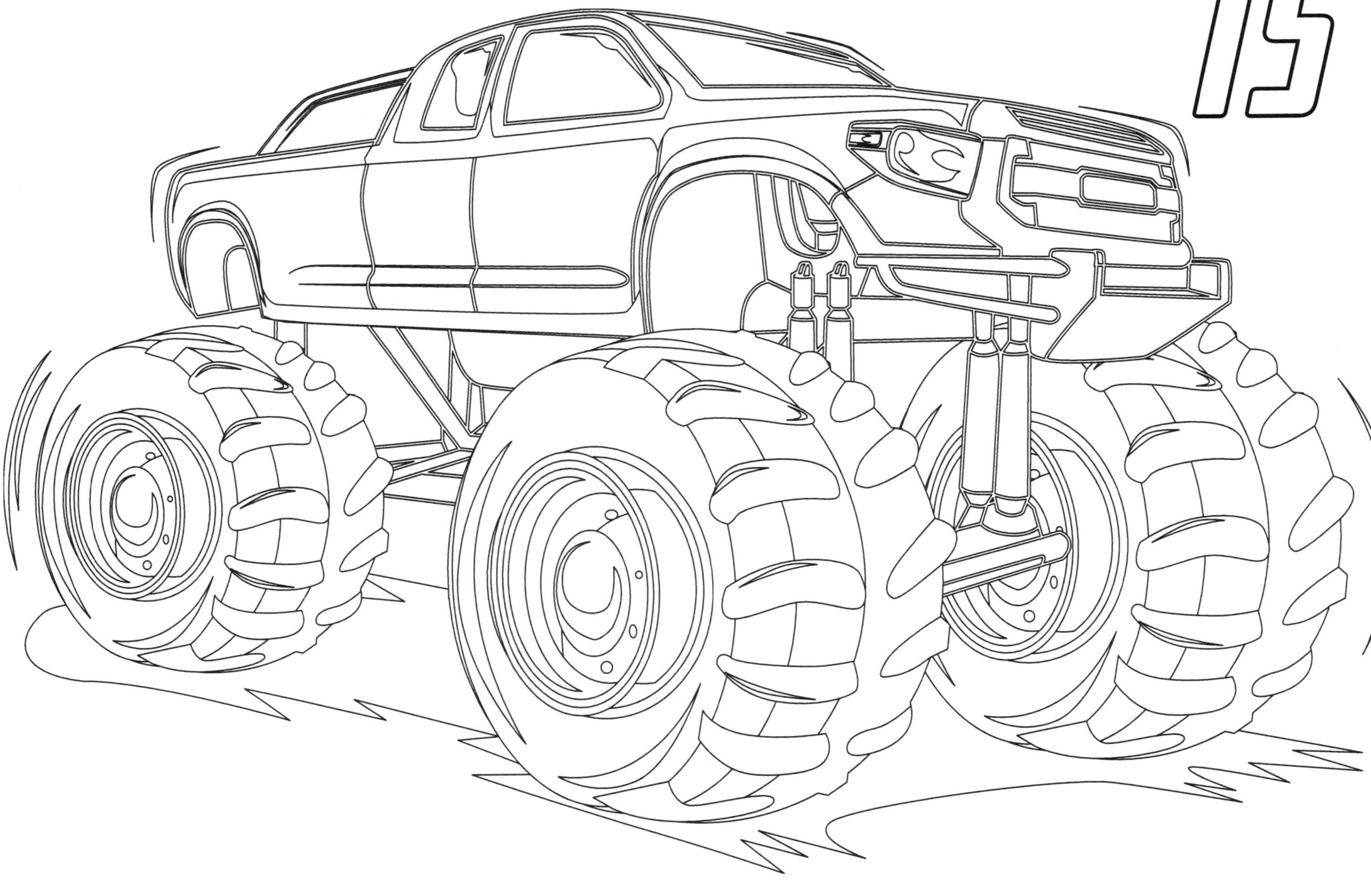

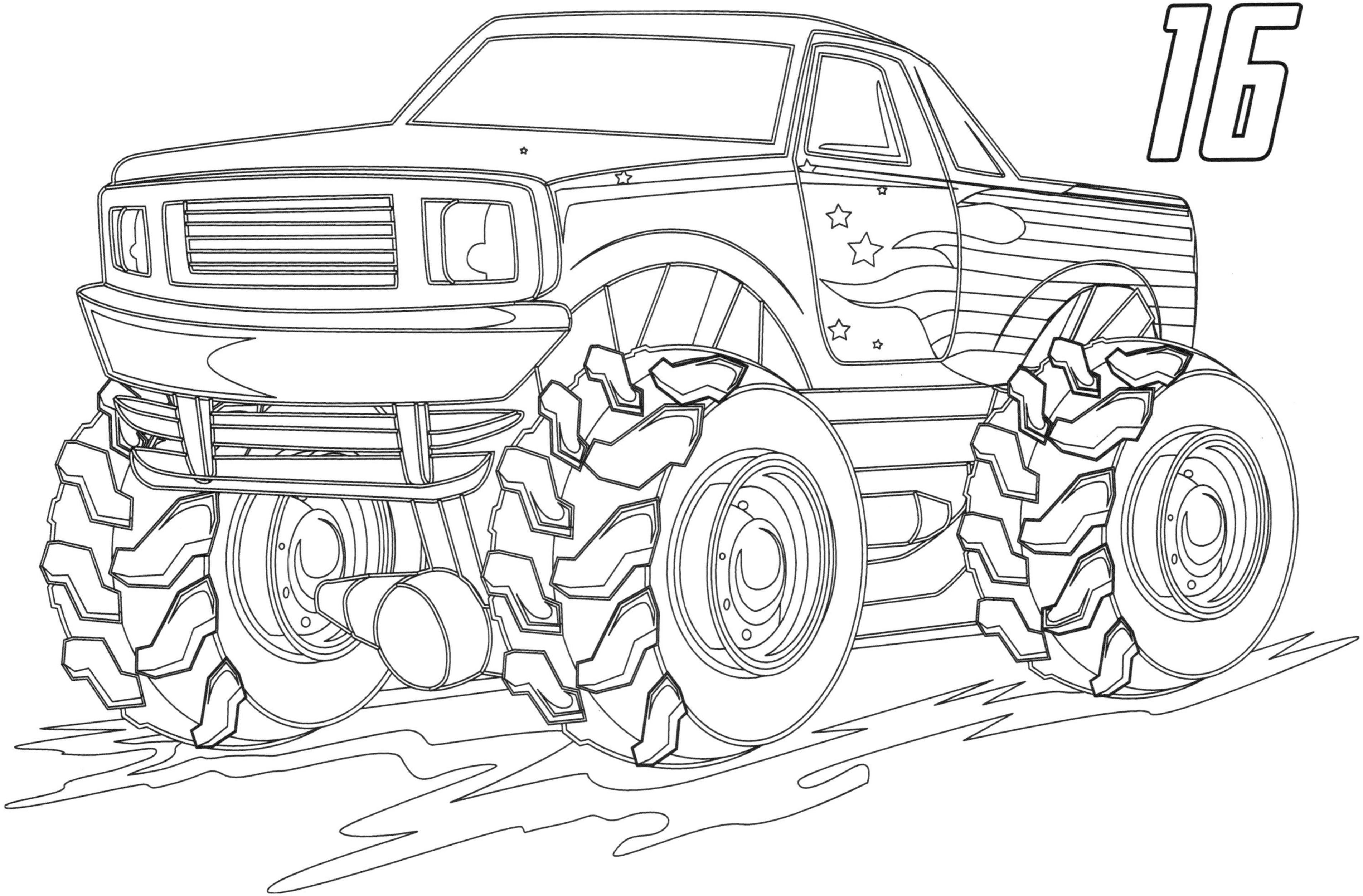
16

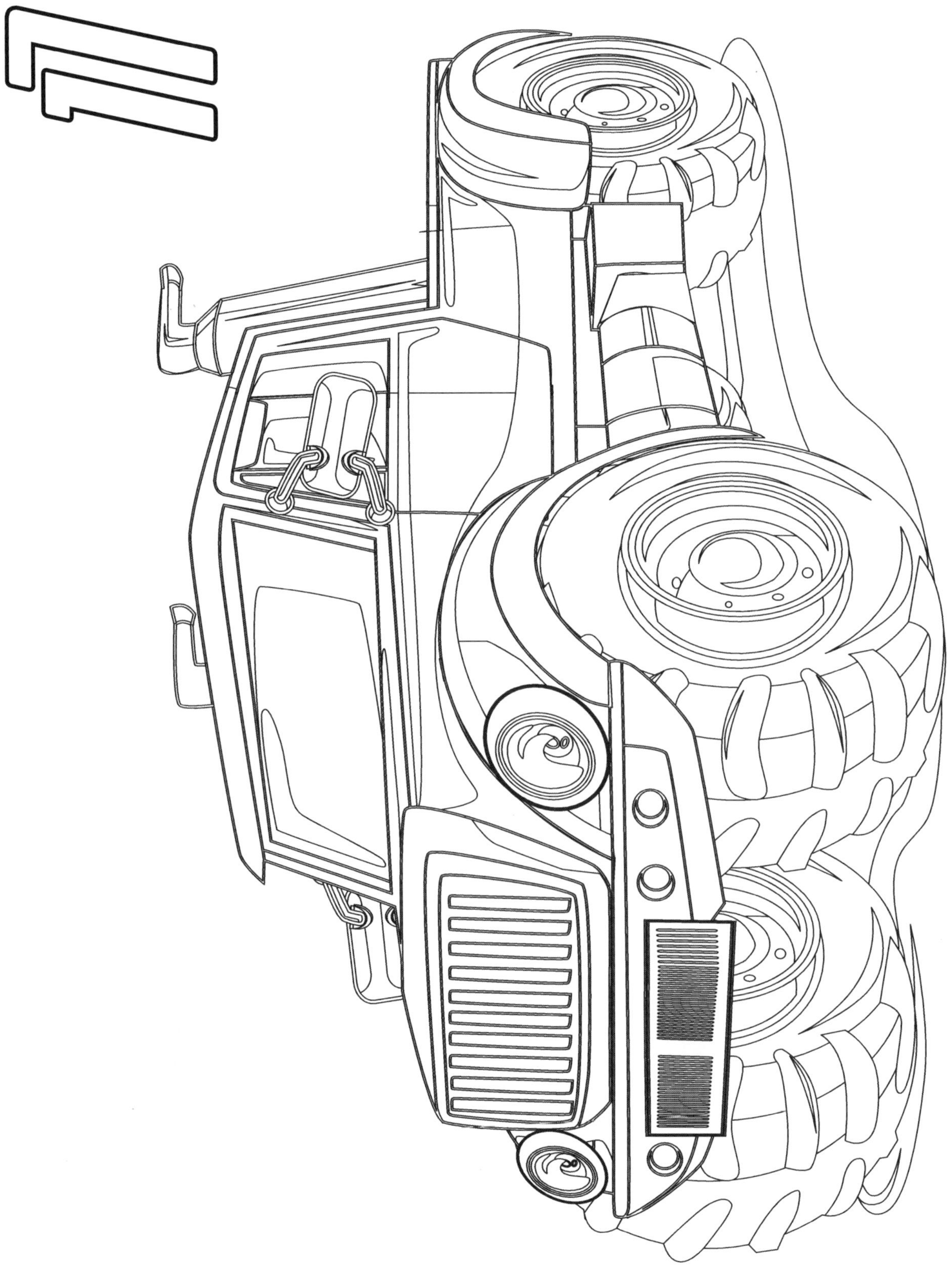
11

18

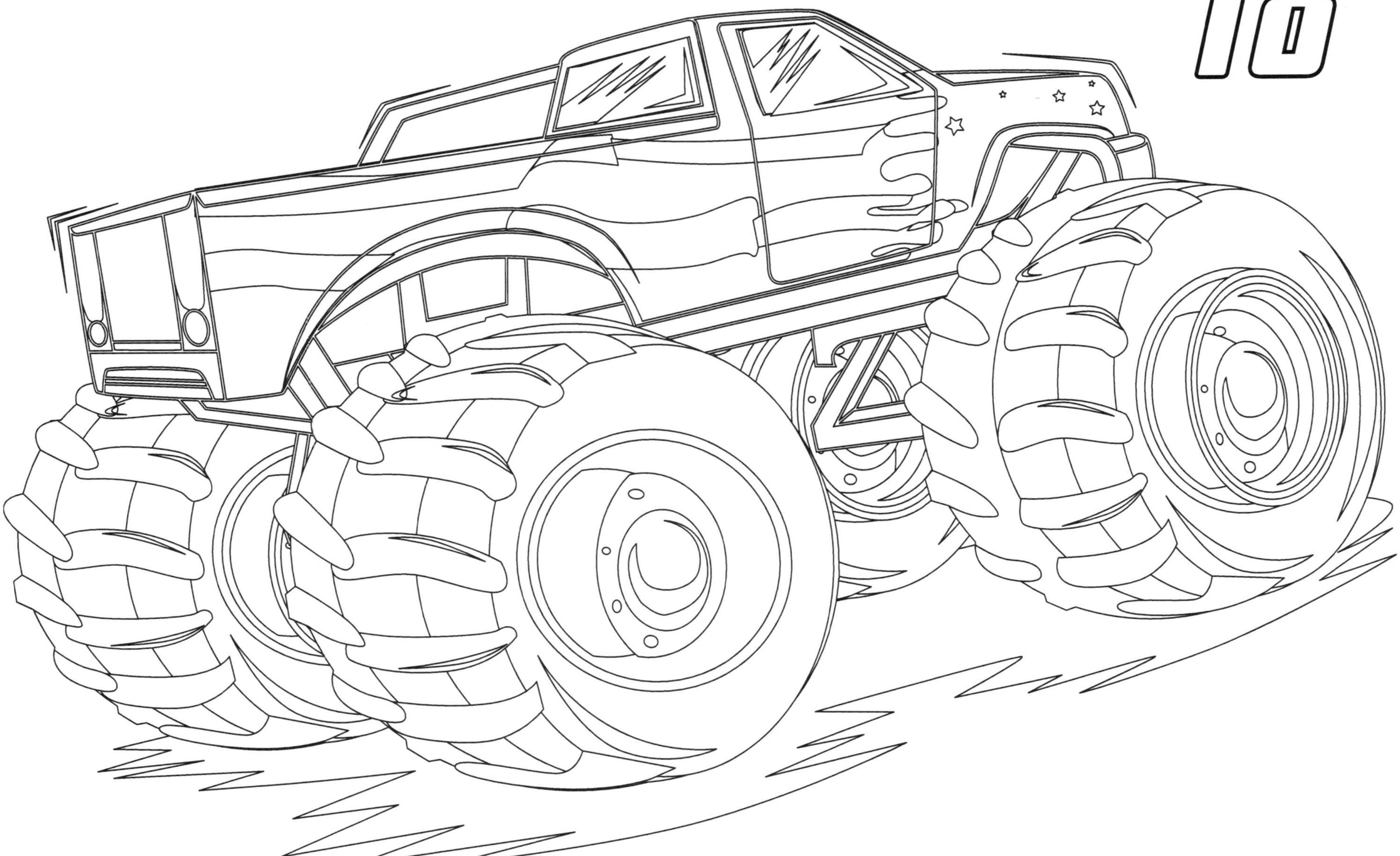

19

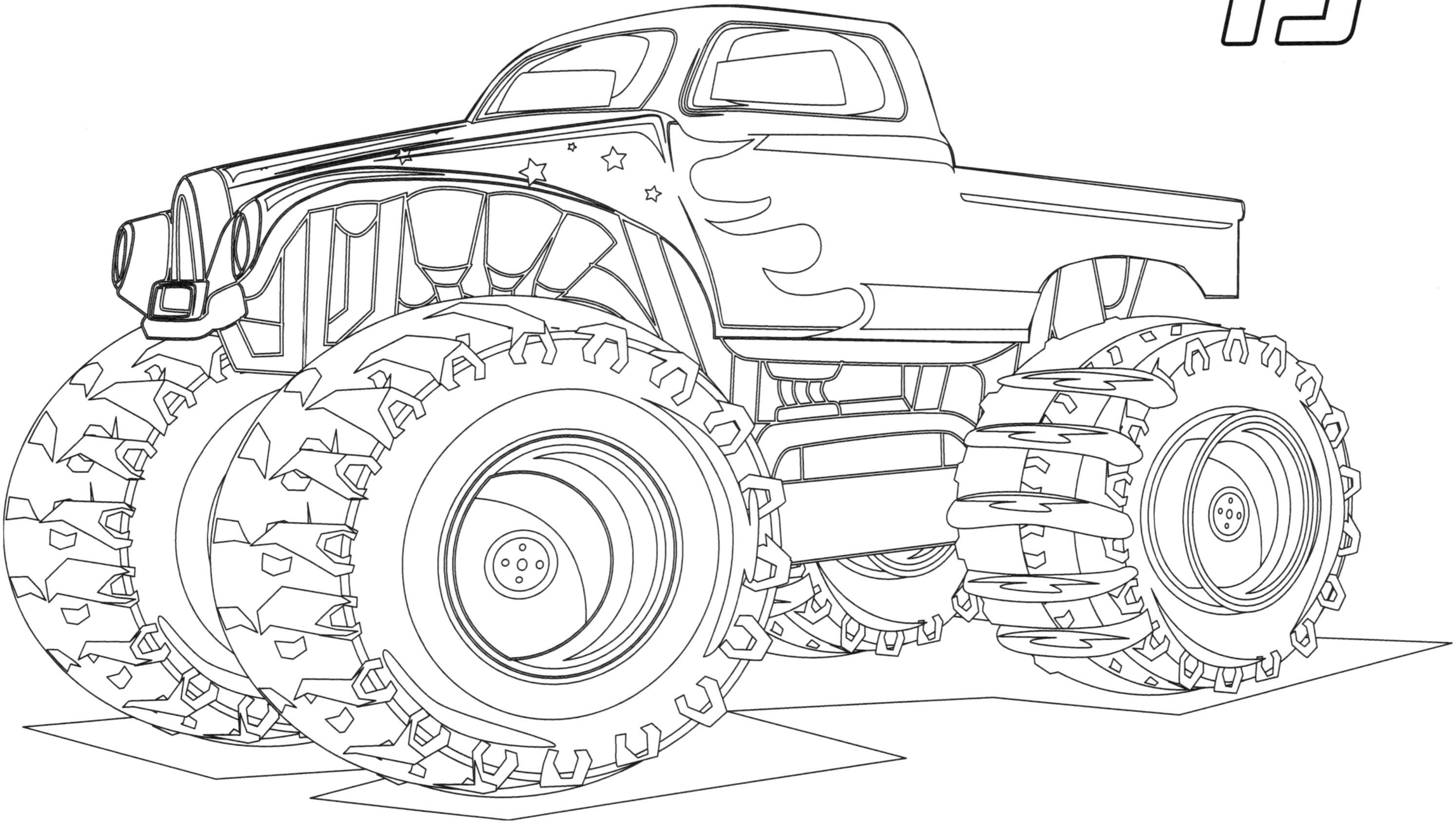

20

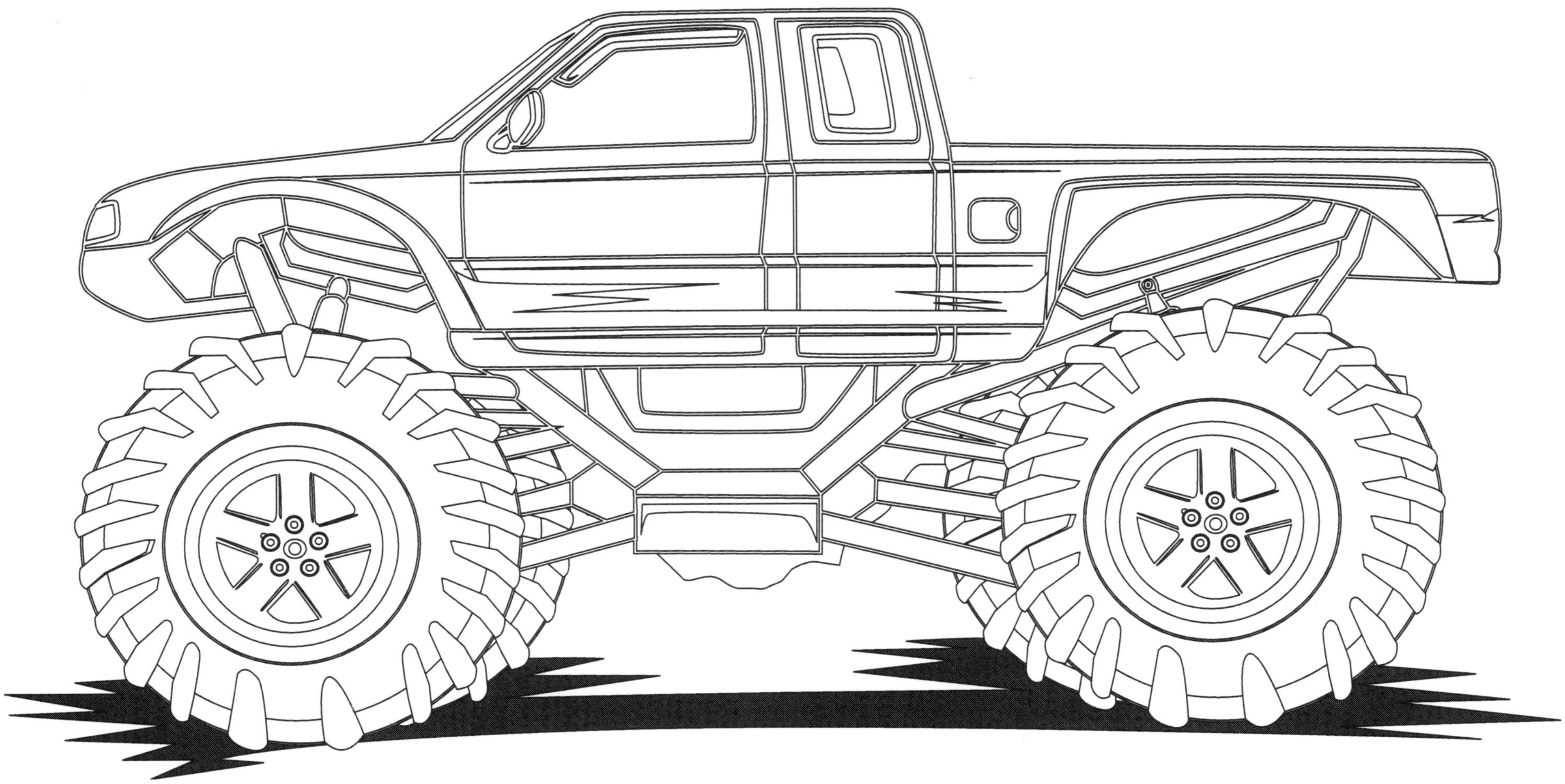

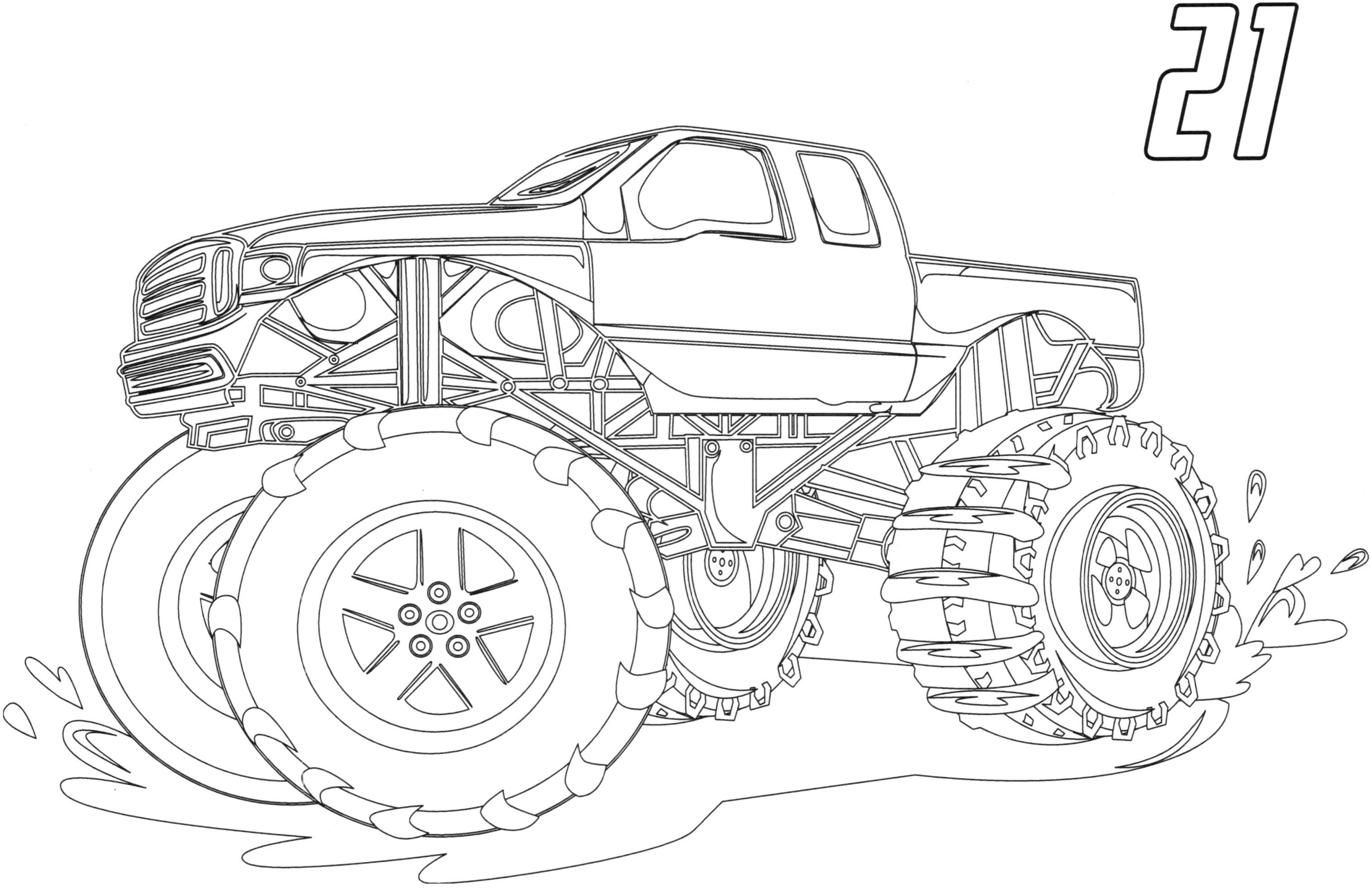
21

Printed in Great Britain
by Amazon

14304225R00027